3510459696

D0569047

PET OWNER'S GUIDE TO THE
RAT

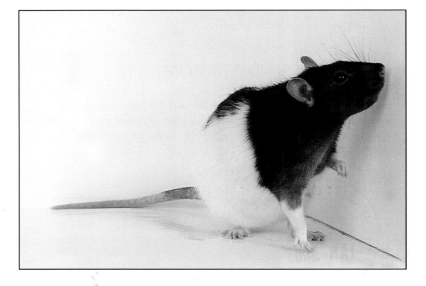

Lorraine Hill

Photography: Amanda Bulbeck

RINGPRESS

ABOUT THE AUTHOR

Lorraine Hill has kept rats for several years, and is an expert on caring for rats in a pet environment. She has bred rats, and has exhibited a number of varieties at shows. Lorraine, a well-known writer on small animals, is a keen campaigner for pet rats, and has introduced many people to them through a series of talks and lectures.

DEDICATION

I would like to dedicate this book to three very special rats – Snoopy, Sylvester, and Champagne Charlie – all now sadly passed on, but who remain in my heart forever. These three rats, beyond all others, taught me how rewarding a relationship with a pet rat can be – and they are still sorely missed.

ACKNOWLEDGMENTS

Many thanks to the various people within the National Rat Fancy Society of the UK who have shared so much knowledge with me over my years of rat-keeping. My thanks also to those who allowed their rats to be photographed, and to Amanda Bulbeck for the delightful photographs.

Published by Ringpress Books Limited,
PO Box 8, Lydney, Gloucestershire,
GL15 6YD, United Kingdom.

First published 1998
©1998 Ringpress Books Limited. All rights reserved

ISBN 1 86054 105 4
Printed in Hong Kong through Printworks Int. Ltd.

HOME
TWEET
HOME

CONTENTS

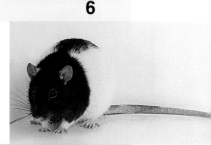

1 Introducing The Rat

Rat is the name given to approximately 1,000 species of rodents, most of which have a long body, a pointed face and a long, hairless or slightly haired tail. However, the number of true rat species of the genus *Rattus* is approximately 80.

The rat is a rodent, having large incisors that continually grow, necessitating gnawing to prevent overgrowing. The word rodent is derived from the Latin word *rodere* meaning "to gnaw". The rat is a pack animal living in large groups, usually closely related, and this allows the rat to adapt and survive in many different environments.

Two species of rats, the Black Rat (*Rattus Rattus*) and the Brown or Norwegian Rat (*Rattus Norvegicus*) are the rats most commonly known because of their association with human history, and the domesticated, or fancy, rat is descended from the Brown Rat.

The Black Rat is 16-22cm in length, with a 17-24cm tail, and grey-black in colour, although

The domesticated or fancy rat is descended from the Brown Rat.

brown variations of *Rattus Rattus* exist. The Black Rat is a good climber and jumper and tends to live above ground level, often in the upper levels of buildings. This has earned it the nickname of the 'roof rat'. The Brown Rat is larger than the Black Rat, being 22-26cm in length with an 18-22cm tail, and is greyish-brown in colour, although blacker variations have occurred in the wild. The Brown Rat prefers to live underground in burrows and tunnels and is a good swimmer, even able to swim underwater for short periods. It can often be found inhabiting sewers and so the Brown Rat is also known as the Sewer Rat. Where the two species inhabit the same territory, the larger Brown Rat will drive the Black Rat out of the area or force it to live in the higher areas of the region.

UNFAIR PREJUDICE

When many people think of rats they think of dirty, disease-riddled, vicious pests, but many species do not deserve this reputation or prejudice, and many species of rat will avoid areas populated by humans. However, the Black Rat and Brown Rat often live in urban areas, and over the years have travelled with humans as stowaways on ships, thus enabling them to spread across the world. In the wild, their ability to gnaw and burrow can make the rat a destructive pest and, because the Black Rat played a part in spreading plague, there is much prejudice against rats in general. It is interesting to note, however, that some countries hold the rat in high regard as a good luck symbol, and in China the rat is considered a symbol of prosperity, being the first animal of the oriental zodiac.

Unfortunately, the prejudice against wild rats is transferred by many people to the domesticated rat which is, actually, clean, intelligent and friendly, and certainly not deserving of any bad

Clean, friendly and intelligent, the rat makes an excellent pet.

reputation and prejudice. In fact, their intelligence and docility make rats highly rewarding and affectionate pets.

HISTORY

Both the Black Rat and the Brown Rat are thought to have originated from Asia, with the Black Rat and, later, the Brown Rat spreading through Europe and then other countries.

The Black Rat was known in Europe around the 4th century and was the host for the bubonic plague in the 6th and 7th centuries and the plague known as the Black Death in the 1300s. However, it was not the rats themselves that carried the plague. Fleas that were carried by the rats and many other animals spread the disease – coupled with bad human hygiene.

The Black Rat reached the USA in the 1500s, travelling across the seas as stowaways, and the Brown Rat first appeared in Europe in 1553 and in America in 1775.

In the early 1800s, rats were captured, kept in captivity and bred in large numbers for use in ratting contests, where terriers competed against each other to kill the most rats within a given time. Each terrier could kill up to 600 rats at one of these ratting contests. In the late 1800s, rats were bred in captivity for use in scientific research into nutrition, genetics, intelligence and disease. Within these scientific laboratories it was noted that the rat was highly suitable as a pet, due to its intelligence and tameness. Over the years, rats have been bred in sterile conditions to be disease-free and the domesticated rat of today certainly should not be compared to its wild ancestors nor to the wild Black Rat.

THE RAT FANCY

The Rat Fancy began in the late 1800s and the keeping and breeding of domestic rats became popular in the early 1900s. The first rat show was held in the UK in 1901. Rat-keeping later declined and this may partly be due to the introduction of 'more appealing' rodents to the pet market. In many people's eyes the rat is not as cute or pretty as other pet rodents such as the hamster, but more and more people are beginning to appreciate that the rat makes an extremely good pet and they are pleasantly surprised by its tameness and intelligence. The keeping of rats as pets is gaining in popularity once again.

Many countries now have Rat Clubs, Rat and Mice Clubs, Rodent Clubs or Pet Clubs, and many of these were set up in the late 1900s. The clubs help to promote the domesticated rat as a pet, to dispel the myths surrounding the rat and to educate rat owners and potential rat owners about their care. Over the years many mutations of colour, coat pattern and coat types have appeared in the domesticated rat and these have been maintained by the Rat Fancy, thus ensuring that, today, there is a good variety of coloured rats available on the pet market.

The domesticated or fancy rat is the result of many years' breeding in captivity and the domesticated rat of today is often bigger than its original wild ancestor, the Brown Rat.

Selective breeding means that the domesticated rat is often bigger than its wild ancestor, the Brown Rat.

2 Acquiring A Pet Rat

It should be remembered that any pet is a living creature and will need care, time and attention. Rats are sociable and affectionate and they need companionship, and the more attention paid to the rat, the more rewarding the relationship with your pet will be – and rats can be very rewarding pets. Rats are now gaining in popularity as pets in many countries, for children and adults alike. They are easy to keep, cost very little in maintenance and take up relatively

Rats are robust enough to be handled by children and make entertaining pets.

little room, making them ideal pets for those living in a small apartment, or those at school or working during the day, as they will easily fit into any household routine.

Rats are clean animals who regularly wash themselves and have very little or no smell. They are nocturnal, becoming more active during the evenings. Rats are colour-blind and their eyesight is poor; they rely mainly on their senses of smell and hearing.

Rats are intelligent, easily trained, lively, agile, docile, friendly and affectionate. They are also playful and good climbers and can provide hours of amusement and companionship.

The rat is a suitable pet for both children and adults, and for young children under supervision. They are big enough and robust enough to be handled by children, although very young children may find them too large to handle unaided. Because they are larger than many other pet rodents they can withstand being handled for longer periods of time and actually enjoy the attention it brings. Care should always be taken that a rat is not squeezed when handled as this could cause the rat to nip, become frightened or be hurt. The typical body size of a full-grown rat is 22cm for a female (doe) weighing approximately 250-300 grams, and 30cm for a male (buck) weighing approximately 450-500 grams. The tail is usually slightly shorter than the body length. The average life-span is two to two-and-a-half years but they can live longer, and up to six years has been known.

WHERE TO BUY

The best place to buy a rat, without doubt, is from a reputable breeder. Rat Clubs, Rodent or Pet Clubs may know of, and be able to put you in touch with, breeders in your area. Alternatively, private breeders may advertise rats for sale locally on shop notice-boards or in local papers. Buying direct from the breeder enables you to see the parents and find out the exact date of birth of the rat, its diet and its likes and dislikes. More and more pet stores are now selling rats, but you will not usually find the wide range of colours or patterns that are available from a private breeder.

If you intend to show your rat at rat shows, it is undoubtedly best to obtain your rat from a specialist breeder who breeds rats for showing. They will be able to advise you on whether a particular rat is a good show prospect or not. For most people, however, a pet store is the most likely place from which to obtain their first rat and the only concern is obtaining a well-mannered, healthy pet. If buying a rat from a pet store, ensure that the rats are housed in clean and adequate conditions, that the condition of the rats appears good and that bucks and does are housed in separate cages.

BUCK OR DOE?

The temperament of males (known as bucks) and females (known as does) with regard to friendliness, intelligence and suitability as a pet is much the same. However, bucks grow much larger and heavier than does and

The buck is larger and heavier, and tends to be more laid back in temperament.

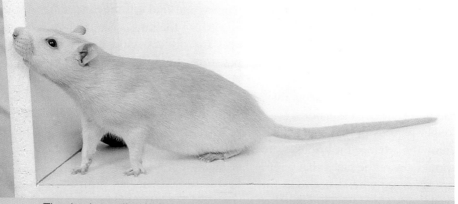

The doe is smaller than the buck and is more active.

will require a larger cage. Bucks are also more laid back and lazy than does, slower-moving and often content with just sitting in your lap during time out of the cage. Does are smaller in length, thinner in the body and are much more active than bucks. They are faster movers and more playful than bucks during times of play out of the cage.

HOW MANY?

Rats are naturally sociable pack animals and so enjoy the company of their own kind. They can be kept in single-sex pairs or groups, either bucks or does. It is possible to keep mixed-sex groups or pairs but these will breed continually from an early age and over-breeding of the does will occur, which could result in health problems, not to mention an abundance of baby rats. Even if it is your intention to buy a buck and doe and breed them, it is best to house them separately and only place them together in the same cage once they reach a suitable age for breeding, rather than housing bucks and does together continually. In any case, before embarking on breeding rats, careful consideration needs to be given to taking this step.

Rats are sociable animals and enjoy each other's company.

A single rat will require a cage with a floor area of approximately 60cm x 30cm and pairs, or groups of rats, should be housed in a cage that allows a space of at least 900 square cm per rat for does, and slightly more for bucks kept together, as they are larger than the does. Rats kept singly will require a lot of owner contact and attention to compensate for the lack of companionship of their own kind, and such rats build strong bonds with their owner.

SELECTING A HEALTHY RAT

It is important when selecting a rat that the bucks and does are housed in different cages. Rats can breed at a very young age and buying a doe from a cage where bucks and does are housed together could mean buying a pregnant doe.

Age: A rat should not be sold under five weeks of age, and the ideal age to buy a rat is between five and ten weeks.

Behaviour: You should look for a rat that is alert, lively and inquisitive when awake but not too nervous.

Health: Check underneath and around the base of the tail to see that there is no wetness or dirtiness as this could be a sign of diarrhoea. Check that the coat is clean, the body is firm, the eyes are clean and bright, the ears are clean and that the rat has no obvious signs of illness – running nose, wheezing, discharge, sneezing, etc. Avoid buying any rat, even a healthy-looking one, from a cage in which one or more rats look to be in bad health.

The best age for buying a rat is between five and ten weeks. This silver chocolate buck is nine weeks old.

Temperament: Ask if you can handle the rat that appeals to you so that you can assess its temperament and suitability as a pet.

SEXING RATS

The breeder or pet store should be able to check the sex of your chosen rat. To sex a rat, place the rat on your hand and gently lift the tail with the other hand to look at the genitals, or hold the rat around the body in an upright position with its underneath facing towards you to view the genitals. On the doe the vaginal opening is very close to the anus – sometimes so close it is difficult to distinguish the two separate vents. On the buck there is a gap of approximately 2cm or more between the penile opening and the anus. However, even on young buck rats the testes are descended and prominent and it is often easy to identify a buck simply by looking at the body profile.

BE PREPARED

It is always a good idea to buy the cage and equipment before buying the rat. You can then have the new home ready beforehand so that the rat can be placed in the cage immediately on arrival home and this will help to keep stress to a minimum.

First, think about where the rat is to be located within the house. The cage should be placed in a room of constant temperature, as sudden changes in temperature can cause health problems. The cage should also be placed away from draughts, and out of direct sunlight, and out of reach of any other pets which may bother or harm the rat. A rat's hearing is very sensitive and a loud environment can cause stress, so the cage should be placed in a relatively quiet area of the house.

Remember, whatever cage you buy for your rat, you should always buy the biggest one you can afford.

A male (buck), pictured left, and a female (doe).

come in a variety of shapes, sizes and colours and are relatively cheap, easy to clean and long-lasting, but are not draught-proof. Cages with high plastic bases will prevent wood shavings and food being kicked out of the cage by the rat. Similar cages designed for keeping guinea pigs or rabbits indoors will also make a suitable rat cage, provided that the bars are not spaced too far apart, allowing the rat to squeeze through, and that they will provide the rat with plenty of space.

MULTI-LEVEL CAGES

A variety of multi-level cages is available, some of which may consist of a plastic base and a rigid wire top with metal or plastic ladders leading up to another floor level within the cage. There are many different shapes and sizes of this type of cage and they can include very nice, built-in features such as little bridges or climbing

Wire cages are often used for rats.

THE BASIC CAGE

There is a variety of rodent cages sold in pet stores. They are of a basic design, and consist of a plastic base and a rigid wire top. Many of these are designed for smaller rodents and are too small for a single rat, but the larger cages are very suitable and some are large enough to accommodate two or more rats. These cages

A multi-level cage provides a variety of locations for your rat.

frames. Some are very reasonably priced, although the more amenities there are, the more expensive the cage. They are suitable for rats, allowing them to display their natural climbing and acrobatic skills. However, some large, full-grown bucks may find the openings between the different floor levels a bit of a squeeze. These cages are long-lasting and relatively easy to clean. Cages with high bases will prevent wood shavings and food being kicked out of the cage by the rat. Enclosed multi-level cages, with interconnecting tubes designed for rodents, are not suitable for rats, as the tubes are too narrow for a full-grown rat to climb through and the cage compartments do not provide enough space for even a young rat.

An aquarium makes an excellent, draught-proof home.

AQUARIUMS

A variety of aquariums is available and these make excellent cages for rats. They are draught-proof and reasonably priced, but glass aquariums can be cumbersome and heavy to clean. As rats are good climbers and can usually jump two feet or more, the aquarium must have a top. Any top should be well ventilated to avoid a build-up of condensation and must be secure and chew-proof to avoid escapes. The plastic aquarium tops are, therefore, totally unsuitable as they do not allow enough ventilation and are very easily destroyed by rats. Some aquariums are designed for rodents and are supplied with metal, or glass, ventilated tops. Alternatively, wire mesh with a wooden frame makes an excellent top for an aquarium, but it must be secure. This can be done by weighting the top down so that the rat is unable to lift it away from the aquarium or by ensuring that the top fits tightly within the aquarium so that it is not pushed away easily. Aquariums are ideal cages for pregnant does, nursing mothers and baby rats.

Wooden cages can be used, but they are often gnawed by the rats.

WOODEN CAGES

A hutch designed for a rabbit or a guinea pig can be used to house a rat, or home-made cages can also be made from wood and wire mesh. However, wooden cages will be gnawed by the rat and so will need constant repair, and there is the danger that the rat could injure itself on damaged and splintered wood. The wood will also soak up the urine, necessitating regular, thorough cage cleaning, so wooden cages are not ideal. The wire mesh of hutches may also be too large to prevent young rats from escaping.

HOME-MADE CAGES

Home-made cages can be constructed from large plastic storage containers. The container will need a secure wire mesh top. These make good cages for nursing mothers, or young rats, as the sides are solid, ensuring that the cage is draught-proof and will not allow young rats to squeeze

Nesting material should be provided.

out. They are easy to clean but, unless made of clear plastic, they do not allow the rat to see out.

WOOD SHAVINGS

A good layer of wood shavings should be used to line the floor of the cage. Shavings, rather than

Wood shavings should be used to line the cage.

sawdust, should be used, as fine sawdust can cause eye and nose irritations. Wood shavings from softwoods such as cedar should be avoided as these contain phenols which can cause health problems in rats. Shavings made from hardwoods such as aspen, or paper products are best. It is always advisable to buy shavings from a pet store rather than from a lumber-yard where you cannot be sure that the wood has not been treated with some chemical which may be harmful to your rat.

NESTING MATERIAL

Rats appreciate some nesting material and hay or shredded paper is best. Straw should not be used, as this is sharp and can cause injury to the rat's eyes or mouth. There is a variety of manufactured bedding materials sold in pet stores. However, any bedding material manufactured from man-made fibres, or any material which is not easily broken or dissolved should not be used as nesting material because it may cause harm to the rat if it is eaten, or injury if the rat gets caught up in the material. Soft, paper-based bedding is ideal, as it is perfectly safe and provides adequate warmth for the rat.

An earthenware bowl cannot be chewed and it is hard to knock over.

FOOD BOWL

An earthenware food bowl is preferable to a plastic bowl, which is easily knocked over and chewed by the rat. A rat will, of course, eat from the floor and this can provide extra stimulation, but it is easier to ensure that your rat is not being overfed if a food bowl is used and refilled daily.

DRINKING BOTTLE

The best way to supply water for your rat is by way of a drinking bottle. This ensures a constant supply of clean water. Drinking bottles with a ball-bearing in the tube are best, as these are less inclined to leak than those without. Drinking bottles come in different sizes. When keeping more than one rat in a cage a larger bottle will be required and it may be necessary to ensure that

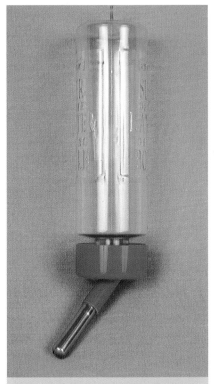

A gravity-fed water bottle will ensure a constant supply of water.

more than one bottle is provided for a cage containing a group of rats.

RAT WHEELS

Many cages have wheels already fitted. If not, it is possible to buy standalone wheels which can be placed inside any cage. Solid wheels are best, but wheels with rungs can have a strip of cardboard woven through them to

A rat wheel provides exercise and entertainment.

prevent the rat's feet slipping through them, or the rat's tail becoming caught, which can result in injury. The rat is likely to chew the cardboard, though, and so it may need replacing regularly to ensure that the rat cannot injure itself on the wheel. Some wheels may squeak after a while and this can be cured by placing a drop of vegetable oil on the axis. Not all rats like to run on a wheel but, for those that do, it provides an excellent means of exercise. The wheels supplied with many cages are designed for smaller rodents and a full-grown rat may find these wheels too small. Many pet stores now sell wheels specifically designed for rats and these are larger than the average rodent wheel.

The agile rat enjoys places where he can climb.

FURNISHING THE CAGE

Rats require some privacy and a box of some kind, within the cage, for nesting in will be appreciated. Small cardboard or wooden boxes can be used, although cardboard boxes may need replacing from time to time if the rat also chews them. PVC drainage tubes also provide some privacy for the rat and toilet roll tubes are ideal for young rats who will also enjoy chewing them to pieces! Ladders, platforms and rope fixed within the cage will all provide the rat with a more stimulating environment and enable the rat to climb and play. Small branches of apple wood placed in the cage will provide the rat with something to gnaw on as well as to climb on.

PLAY AREAS

Many owners like to build their rats play areas and these can be easily made with simple, inexpensive items and some imagination. Aquariums or plastic storage boxes, filled three-quarters full with shavings or peat, make excellent burrowing boxes. Alternatively, aquariums or plastic storage boxes containing mazes, objects to climb on, or tunnels, also provide fun play areas for rats.

Hidey-holes are always a favourite.

TRAVELLING BOXES

There may be occasions when it will be necessary to travel with your rat – for example to the vet or to a show, and it may not be practicable to take the rat in its cage. Small plastic pet carriers or plastic aquariums are available in most pet stores and these provide an excellent way of transporting small pets.

Fruit tree branches can be used for climbing – and for gnawing.

3 Caring For Your Rat

Rats are thought of as scavengers, and, certainly, they are not the fussiest of feeders. However, as with all pets, it is important to provide a correct well-balanced diet in order to ensure good health.

DIETARY REQUIREMENTS

Many pet shops now sell dry pellets specifically designed for rats and mice. 'Rodent blocks' or 'lab blocks' available in some pet stores also provide a suitable diet for rats. Alternatively, pre-prepared hamster mixes will also provide the correct dietary requirement for your rat. Your rat's diet can also be supplemented by a variety of treats.

FEEDING

Rat pellets, rodent blocks, lab blocks, hamster mix, or a combination of these, should form the main part of your rat's diet. Hamster mixes consist of grains, cereals, nuts and seeds such as

A well-balanced diet is essential for your rat's health and well-being.

Complete feeds will supply the basic needs.

crushed oats, barley, wheat, sunflower seeds, peanuts, maize, flaked peas and biscuit. Some mixes are not always of good quality; look for a mix that has plenty of ingredients and an even quantity of each of them. If you buy your rat from a breeder, find out what food the rat is used to and, if possible, feed the same or a similar food. If you wish to change the food your rat is fed, do this gradually, feeding a bit of both the old and new food at first so that your rat does not have a sudden change of diet which could cause a stomach upset. Gradually increase the amount of the new pellet or mix and reduce the amount of the old food over a few days, until you are feeding just the new pellets or mix.

GREEN FOOD

Most rats will appreciate some 'green' food, but any vegetables and fruit should be introduced gradually to the diet in small amounts, as too much too soon can cause diarrhoea. Most rats will normally eat carrot, cabbage, broccoli, beans, parsley, cauliflower leaves and stalks, banana, grapes, tomatoes, pear, swede, peas and apple. Although some rats will eat Brussels sprouts

Rats appreciate 'green' foods as part of their diet.

Vegetables provide vitamins and minerals.

and spinach, not all will appreciate them because of the strong taste. Any vegetable or fruit should be clean, dry, pesticide-free and free from frost damage. Individual rats will have different tastes and so not all rats will enjoy the same foods.

RAT TREATS

There are a variety of rat treats, or rodent treats, sold in pet stores and most rats relish these. Some treats sold in pet shops are designed to be hung from the top of the cage and these provide stimulation as well as food for the rat. Rats will eat a variety of foods and can be fed most table scraps including meat and fish. Other treats can include dog and cat biscuits, nuts, bread, scrambled or boiled egg, plain biscuit or cake. Common sense should be used

and spicy or fattening foods high in sugar content should be avoided. It should always be remembered that any such treats are just that – treats, and should be fed as an occasional supplement to the rat's basic pellet or dry mix diet. Another treat that is enjoyed by rats, and which is particularly helpful to nursing mothers and

Crushed dog biscuits provide good gnawing material.

young rats, providing plenty of vitamins, is food designed for human babies. Many rats prefer the savoury baby foods such as 'chicken casserole' or 'pork and vegetables' to the sweet 'pudding' varieties.

QUANTITY

Rats require approximately 30 grams of food per day, although they will often eat more if it is provided. Too much food can lead to obesity, especially if the rat picks out its favourite ingredients, which are likely to be the most fattening. Obesity can lead to health problems and may shorten the rat's lifespan. A good handful of food with some treats each day is sufficient.

BRAN/OAT MASH

A bran or oat mash can be made with milk, porridge oats and bran, and rats will enjoy this as a supplement to their diet. This is a very good supplement for a pregnant doe, a nursing mother and young baby rats. Muesli soaked in milk is also enjoyed by rats, as are some breakfast cereals (dry or in milk), but be careful not to feed too much sweetened food.

WATER

Clean water should always be available and therefore it is important to ensure that the drinking bottle is never empty. Rats usually drink approximately 60ml of water per day but may

Rats that are kept together should be of a similar size and age. These agouti bucks are ten weeks old.

Give your rat a chance to explore his cage.

drink more in hot weather, or less if green food is fed. Vitamin drops, which can be purchased in pet stores, can be added to the water to ensure that your rat is receiving all the vitamins needed.

SETTLING IN

The cage will need to be prepared by covering its floor with a thick layer of wood shavings and placing a pile of bedding in one corner of the cage or in the nesting box. Fill the drinking bottle with water and, if the cage has wire sides, fix it to the side of the cage at a height the rat will be able to reach comfortably. Aquariums designed for housing rodents may have a fixture for attaching water bottles. Otherwise, water bottles can be attached to aquarium sides by using self-adhesive Velcro pads, although this is not ideal, as the

rat is likely to climb the water bottle and may pull it away from the wall of the aquarium. Water bottles designed to be hung from a wire are much better, as the wire can be hooked over the side of the aquarium or the water bottle can be hung from the aquarium top. Once the water bottle is in place, check by running your finger over the spout that water is getting through. Place the food bowl and food in the cage, with any other equipment such as a rat wheel, tubes, rope, ladders, etc. and the cage is ready for its new occupant.

On arrival home, gently take your new rat from the carrying box and place the rat in the cage, ensuring that any cage doors are firmly shut or aquarium lids firmly secured. Your new rat is sure to explore the cage, and may take some time to settle down to rest. It is best to leave your new rat in peace for the first day or two so that it has a chance to become familiar with the new environment, its smells and sounds, and to feel confident in its new home. Speak gently to your rat at feeding time, giving it the chance to become familiar with your voice, and allow it to sniff your hand so that it becomes familiar with your scent.

If you are buying more than one rat to live together, it is best to buy them at the same time – they need not be related but they should be roughly the same size and age and, in any case, should be under ten weeks of age. It is often difficult to introduce a young rat to an older rat, or two or more older rats to each other, particularly if one or more has become used to living on its own, and so rats are best paired or grouped when young. They should then be placed in their new home together.

If the rats were not previously living together, or were living together as part of a larger group, there may be some squabbling as they get used to each other, and they will wish to establish an order of dominance. One rat may stand on its hindlegs and 'throw' the other to the floor on its back and lick or bite at its belly, or push the other one into a corner of the cage and sniff at its genitals. This is the rat's way of asserting its dominance. The submissive rat may squeal a little during this process but peace and tranquillity will usually follow. Unless constant noisy fighting is occurring, it is best to leave them to sort this out without interference. Does, particularly, may be very vocal during these squabbles to determine dominance but observation will usually confirm that the physical contact is minimal. If serious or prolonged fighting does occur, it may be necessary to put the rats into separate cages, but the need for this when introducing young rats to each other is rare.

GENERAL CARE

Your rat is mainly nocturnal and so will sleep for most of the day and become more active in the evening. It is therefore best to feed your rat in the evening. By feeding a little earlier each evening it is possible to 'train' your rat to awaken a little earlier. If you wish to wake your rat at feeding time, this is best done by tapping on the side of the cage – the rat will take a little while to wake fully. Poking

A rat will groom himself, rather like a cat does.

a sleeping rat usually results in only one outcome – a bite! Being nocturnal, the evening is also the time when your rat will eagerly want to play and share your companionship.

CLEANING THE CAGE

The cage should be cleaned once a week, throwing away all the old wood shavings, leftover food and any soiled bedding – any clean bedding can be returned to the clean cage along with some fresh bedding. If it is necessary to wash the base of the cage, this can be done using a weak solution of washing-up liquid and water, rinsing thoroughly afterwards, or using a disinfectant specifically designed for the cleaning of small animal cages. The water in the drinking bottle should be replaced with fresh water and the food dish refilled. It may be necessary, between cage cleanings, to remove any perishable foods which have not been eaten, in order to avoid moist food becoming mouldy or starting to rot, so ensure 'green' food is removed if left uneaten at the end of each day.

GROOMING

Rats wash themselves rather like a cat does – you will notice that your rat will lick its coat and also lick its paws or feet and then scratch or rub its coat. It is not necessary to bath your rat, but many owners do bath their rats before entering them in a show. If you do wish to bath your rat this is best done by placing your rat in a shallow bowl of lukewarm water and gently pouring water over the rat's body. The rat, once wet, can be gently washed using mild baby shampoo, being careful to avoid the head and eyes. The rat should be rinsed thoroughly with clean, lukewarm water to remove all shampoo, and then thoroughly dried to avoid catching a chill. The rat can be dried by rubbing firmly with a towel. A hairdryer can be used to finish drying the rat off, but this should be on a cool setting and held at a good distance from the rat to avoid overheating.

The more you handle your rat, the tamer he will become.

HANDLING YOUR RAT

It may take a while for your rat to become accustomed to being handled, but many people are surprised at how tame a young rat can be. In fact, they can be much less inclined to bite than many other types of small rodents sold as pets, and this docility surprises many first-time rat owners. The rat will soon become accustomed to you and your voice and, once your rat has become used to its new surroundings, it is best to start handling by simply allowing the rat to sniff your hand, and by stroking the rat while it is in its cage. Talking gently at the same time will reassure your rat that you mean no harm. Offer your rat a food treat direct from your hand and give your rat the chance to smell you and get used to your scent. Once your rat is happy to be stroked in the cage it will usually happily step onto your hand and climb up your arm. Rats are naturally inquisitive and love to explore – and that includes you! They will climb all over you.

If you wish to remove your rat from its cage it is often easier to pick it up, if the top of the cage can be removed, rather than try to remove your rat from the cage through a small door. You can then slide one hand under the rat's body while placing the other hand on top of its body and lifting it out. Do not lift your rat by its tail – this can damage it, particularly if held towards the end of the tail. If you have difficulty in catching your rat you can gently hold your rat's tail at the base to restrain it, but you should use the other hand, placed under the body, to actually lift the rat from the cage. Avoid sudden movements as these will startle your rat. Be careful not to lift your rat too high as, if it should jump, it may injure itself or escape. At first, always handle your rat while you are sitting so that, should it jump, it will land in your lap. Let your rat walk from one hand to another and, if it should try to jump, it is often better to let it do so and then gently pick it up again, rather than try to hold on to it, which may frighten it – never squeeze your rat. Rats are very inquisitive and your rat is likely to climb all over you, getting to know you better. With gentle, regular handling, your rat will become very tame in a short space of time.

Standing and staring: Something has caught his attention.

RUNNING LOOSE

You may wish to let your rat run loose during your periods of play but this must always be done under supervision. Rats, particularly does, are quick movers and can run under furniture before you realise. Loose rats can also chew through electric cabling and furniture, and squeeze through small gaps in furniture, etc., so a loose rat may become lost, or cause damage to furniture or itself if left unsupervised.

Also, before letting your rat run loose, you should ensure that any other pets that may frighten or hurt the rat are away from the area. Once your rat has become familiar with you, and accepts you as its friend, it is likely to follow you or stay near you when out of the cage and will enjoy playing games, or simply sitting with you, enjoying being petted.

It is not wise to let your rat run

CARING FOR YOUR RAT

loose outdoors as it could easily be harmed by other animals or birds (particularly any birds of prey); it could easily escape or eat unsuitable plants which may be poisonous, or have been fouled by other animals or treated with insecticides.

LEVELS OF RESPONSE

Rats are highly intelligent and this is what sets them apart from the many other pet rodents. Their intelligence makes them highly rewarding and fun pets. Your rat will soon become accustomed to your voice, and calling your rat by its name at feeding time will enable your rat to become familiar with its name. After a while your rat will learn to come when called and rewarding this with a treat will help with the training. This can be an invaluable trick if your rat escapes, as all you need do is simply call its name and it should re-appear!

By repeating and rewarding actions with treats you can train your rat to perform a variety of 'tricks'. Treats can be used to lead the rat into performing the actions required and, by giving a vocal command at the same time, rats will soon make the connection

between the vocal command and action in the same way that a dog does. In this way rats can be trained to do such tricks as climbing onto their owner's shoulder, going back into their cage, or climbing up to their owner's shoulder from the ground. It is best to wear trousers for this trick as rat claws on uncovered legs can be sharp! Rats are also playful and they will enjoy playing games, chasing bits of rope or string, much like the games kittens will play.

ADDITIONAL CHECKS

Each time you clean the cage, check that your rat's droppings appear normal – runny droppings may indicate diarrhoea and a lack of droppings may indicate constipation. Check that your rat appears healthy, its body is firm to the touch and there are no signs of illness, e.g. running nose, wheezing, runny eyes, wetness underneath, etc. You should also check from time to time that your rat's teeth are not becoming overgrown.

RAT BEHAVIOUR

TEETH CHATTERING
Teeth chattering is a sign of

pleasure and is your rat's way of purring. Sometimes you may also feel the rat gently vibrate throughout its body and the rat may half-close its eyes. This shows that your rat is content and happy.

STANDING AND STARING
The rat stands on its hindlegs with an inquisitive expression, nose lifted and whiskers twitching – something has caught its attention. It is listening intently to some sound, or has smelt something interesting. A rat's hearing is very acute and it can hear sounds beyond our human hearing. Its sense of smell is also very good.

HIGH-PITCHED SQUEAL
There may be times when your rat will produce a short high-pitched squeal – this is an expression of alarm, and something may have surprised or shocked the rat. Young rats may let out short squeals when first picked up. Speak to the rat to reassure it.

FIGHTING/PLAYING
Rats are playful and will also

establish an order of dominance. Most fighting is therefore either play, or 'putting the other one in its place', and nothing to be concerned about. This play, or dominance establishment, usually only lasts a few minutes and may be accompanied by short squeals. Often one rat will push another to the floor, or into the corner of the cage, asserting its dominance. However, older rats, if introduced to each other, may fight, particularly if they are used to living alone, and serious fighting could occur with much jumping about and squealing. Injury could result if they are not separated. Introducing two older rats to each other is not easily done.

GNAWING
A rat's teeth grow continually and so it is necessary for your rat to gnaw in order to prevent the teeth from overgrowing. There are wood chews, etc. sold in pet stores

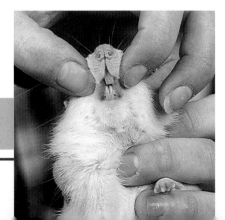

Rats' teeth grow all the time, so it is important to provide gnawing material.

Beware! Rats are great escape artists.

specifically for this purpose but a rat will also gnaw on hard dog biscuits, apple wood or the bars of its cage.

ESCAPES AND CAPTURES

Rats are good at escaping – their intelligence, agility and strength can be put to good use in escape attempts! Once out, they usually travel alongside walls and may head for somewhere dark, such as under furniture. If your rat escapes, ensure all outside doors are shut and that all other pets are kept out of the area. Escaped rats do not usually travel far, and there is always a good chance that your rat is still in the room in which the cage is located, so shut the door to confine the rat to that room. If your rat has been trained to come

to call, you may only need to call its name for it to re-appear. Alternatively, most rats will return to their cage around feeding time, so ensure that your rat is able to reach its cage and that the cage door remains open. At the normal feeding time, place some tasty treats in the cage to entice your rat back into it. If all else fails, search under the furniture and in any other dark areas; often droppings can be found which will indicate the whereabouts of your rat.

4 Colours And Coat Types

Over the years many colour mutations have occurred, with a lot of them appearing in the early years of the keeping of domestic rats. Combining these mutant genes has created further colours and there are many different colours available today.

COLOURS

The original wild colouring of the domestic rat is the Agouti, the natural colouring of the Brown Rat. Other common colours often seen in pet stores include Black, Mink, Champagne and Albino.

Agouti: The natural wild colour.

Cinnamon: Darker hairs are ticked through the coat.

AGOUTI, being the natural wild colour, is often seen in pet stores. It is a dark rich brown, with black hairs ticked through the coat giving it a 'speckled' appearance. A rat with this colour coat has black eyes.

BLACK was a very early colour mutation and appeared in the 19th century. Such rats are jet black with black eyes – these are particularly hard to breed as most Black rats have a sprinkling of silver hairs through the coat. To obtain a good-quality Black rat it will be necessary to find a specialist breeder.

CINNAMON appeared in 1925 and is cinnamon brown in colour with dark brown hairs ticked through the coat, giving it a slightly speckled appearance, and the eyes are black. The Cinnamon can also sometimes be found in pet stores.

Silver fawn: Bright ginger with silver hairs throughout the coat.

SILVER FAWN occurred in 1910 and is a very striking colour, being bright ginger with silver hairs sprinkled through the coat; the belly may be slightly paler and the eyes are red. The Silver Fawn can occasionally be found in pet stores.

MINK appeared in the early 1900s and is an attractive colour, being mid grey/brown with a slight purple tinge. The eyes are black. The Mink is a colour that is often seen in pet stores.

Mink: This colour has a faint purple tinge.

Champagne: Dull cream with bright-red eyes.

CHAMPAGNE is bred from Black and Silver Fawn and is a pale off-white or dull cream in colour with distinctive red eyes.

ALBINO is pure white in colour with red eyes. The Albino appeared in 1810 and was the first colour mutation of the domestic rat to appear. It can often be found in pet stores.

BLACK EYED WHITE is white in colour with black eyes. The Black Eyed White is not a true white and so many have a small patch or spot of colour on the head. This colour is not often seen in pet stores and is most often obtained from a specialist breeder.

CHOCOLATE is a dark chocolate brown in colour with black eyes. These are rarely seen and can usually only be obtained from a specialist breeder.

BLUE is a particularly attractive colour and usually only obtainable from a specialist breeder. It is a striking blue grey in colour with black eyes.

SIAMESE is similar in colouring to a Siamese cat and has a light beige body with dark brown around the nose and around the base of tail and the eyes are red. The Siamese appeared in 1979 and they are sometimes found in pet stores but mostly obtainable from specialist breeders.

Silver Grey: Jet black with silver hairs.

HIMALAYAN appeared in 1972 and has a white body with dark brown colouring around the nose, feet and tail, with red eyes. They are not often seen in pet stores, but can be obtained from a specialist breeder.

SILVER GREY is jet black with silver hairs sprinkled through the coat. Many Black rats gain silver hairs in the coat as they grow older and the amount of silver hairs in the coat varies from one rat to another. The eyes are black. The Silver Grey is often seen in pet stores.

BUFF is pale beige in colour with black eyes, and is not seen in pet stores but is only available from specialist breeders.

TOPAZ is rich golden in colour with silver hairs sprinkled through the coat and dark ruby-red eyes.

Topaz: Golden with silver hairs. Note the ruby-red eyes.

PATTERNS

Pattern mutations produce a white pattern which can be combined with any of the colours.

Berkshire: A coloured body with white belly and feet.

IRISH has a coloured body and a small white triangle on the chest and white feet. The Irish has been known since the early 1800s. It is particularly hard to breed a perfect triangle and so many Irish rats may have a few white hairs on the chest or a patch of any shape. To obtain a nicely marked Irish it will be necessary to locate a specialist breeder.

BERKSHIRE appeared in 1957 and has a coloured body and a white belly and feet. Sometimes the white may not extend across the entire belly, or the line along the sides separating the coloured top coat from the white belly may not be clear and straight. The Berkshire is often found in pet stores but may not have perfect markings.

HOODED is the most common pattern variety and it is often seen in pet stores. It appeared in the mid-1800s and the rat has a coloured head and shoulders. The body is white with a coloured line down the centre of the back to the tail. Sometimes the coloured area down the spine may be incomplete or may only consist of a few spots of colour. The Black Hooded and Agouti Hooded are

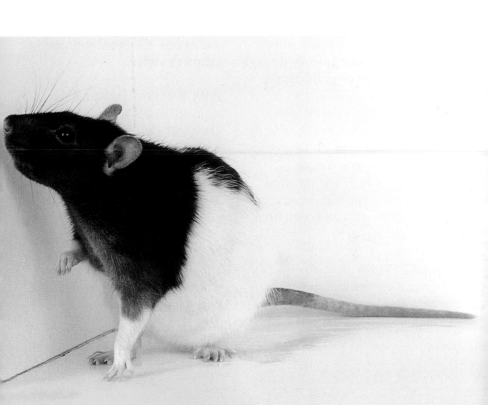

Hooded: A white body with coloured head and shoulders.

very common and are often seen in pet stores. To obtain a nicely-marked Hooded, however, may require contacting a specialist breeder.

CAPPED has a completely white body and only the head is coloured. These can sometimes be found in pet stores but are most often obtained from specialist breeders.

VARIEGATED is white with coloured spots or patches. The head and centre of the back is usually heavily coloured with the sides having more definite spots or patches of colour. They are rarely found in pet stores.

PEARL is a coloured rat with a 'pearl' appearance and is particularly attractive. The Pearl appeared in 1978. The colour is much diluted, as the base of the hairs are pale and many white hairs are sprinkled evenly through the coat. This gives the rat the overall appearance of a white rat with some hairs tipped with colour. The amount of colouring can vary from one rat to another. The most common is the Cinnamon Pearl and the Mink Pearl. These are seldom seen in pet stores but can be obtained from specialist breeders.

COAT TYPES

Over the years coat mutations have also appeared. These mutations affect the coat of the rat and can be combined with any colour or pattern.

REX is a curly-coated rat and appeared in 1976. The hairs are lifted and curled and appear softer than normal. The hairs on bucks are usually more curled and some bucks can look like woolly sheep! The whiskers are curly. The Rex is not often seen in pet stores.

HAIRLESS: The Hairless rat is self-explanatory and not a variety which will appeal to all. It is not kept in all countries.

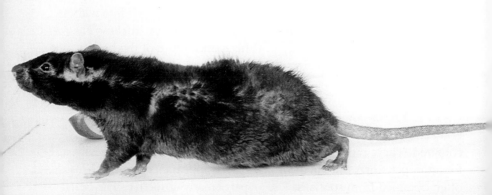

Rex: The hairs are curled and are softer in texture.

5 Breeding Rats

Many owners at some time or other decide that they would like to breed their rats. This may be because they want a baby rat from their much-loved rat, one to keep when their rat dies, or in an effort to make a profit from keeping their pets.

Firstly, before considering breeding, you need to consider what you will do with the surplus babies. You may only want to keep one or two from the litter but it should be borne in mind that, although the average number in a litter for a rat is eight, they can have up to 22 babies and so you may have a large number of baby rats to find homes for.

Secondly, if it is your intention to breed rats for profit, it should be noted that breeding pets rarely results in a profit as there are additional costs involved. To breed rats, additional cages and water bottles are needed, extra food and wood shavings will be

Think carefully before you get involved in breeding rats.

required. In addition, to preserve the good health of the doe and to ensure the best litter results, does should not be bred from more than two or three times in their lifetime.

Local pet stores may be willing to take, or buy, surplus babies from you, or you may have friends that would like to have a baby rat from you. Alternatively, there may be a rat show where you could sell some babies, but you should check this out *before* you breed your rats. Pet stores often have their own regular suppliers and are not willing to take one-off or intermittent litters from pet owners. Even if they do, they will not pay a high price for the rats (usually only about a quarter or a third of the price that they sell them at in the store). You should also bear in mind that not every pet store will buy or sell rats. If you are unable to make plans for the potential large number of surplus babies, then it is best not to breed your rats.

THE AGE FOR BREEDING

A doe can breed at an early age, often as young as five to six weeks of age, which is why, when buying a rat, you should ensure that bucks and does are housed separately.

However, it is best to breed a doe for the first time when she is three to four months of age, as this has given her time to mature, gain condition, and obtain full growth. To breed from a doe younger than that could result in the doe having difficulty producing milk for the litter, resulting in poorly-conditioned babies, or the doe could be reluctant to care for the litter due to her immaturity. Breeding at an early age can also stunt the growth of the doe, or cause the doe's condition to deteriorate, leading to health problems due to the strain put on her during her own development. This, in turn, can lead to a shortened lifespan.

Breeding a doe for the first time at over six months of age can sometimes result in difficulties giving birth and so is best avoided. Once bred at three to four months of age, the doe should then be given at least two to three months to recover condition before breeding again. Does are usually fertile until approximately 15-18 months of age.

Bucks can be used for breeding from as young as five to six weeks of age but because of their small size at this age compared to a full-grown doe, it is better to use a buck that is a little older. Bucks are generally fertile for the majority of their life.

THE RIGHT CONDITIONS

Any rat that is bred from, or bought with breeding in mind, should be of the highest quality and of good health. You may only be interested in breeding rats as pets and not for showing, and so colour may be unimportant, but the size, health, condition and temperament of any rat should be considered before breeding. Small, under-conditioned rats, or rats with any health problems, should not be bred from and careful thought should be given to breeding from any rat that has a bad temperament, as these traits can all be passed on to any babies. If breeding from a rat which has an undesirable trait such as bad temperament or nervousness, it is important that the rat is paired with a rat which has the desired qualities in abundance i.e. a docile temperament, confidence, etc. to counteract the bad traits passed from the other parent. Any rat with a genetic deformity, or any illness, should not be bred from as this is likely to be passed to the babies.

THE DOE IN SEASON

The doe will usually come into season every five days and will be noticeably more active at this time. As rats are nocturnal, does usually come into season mid-evening and this may last through until the morning. Although rats will usually breed all through the year, some does may stop coming into season completely during the colder and darker winter months. This can be helped by leaving a light on during the day and evening and feeding greens – in short, trying to persuade the doe that it is actually summer.

A doe in season is often jumpier and more active than usual and may flap her ears rapidly. If sharing the cage with other does, a doe in season may stand still and lift her rear end or move her tail to one side when other does are near her. Often the other does will mount the doe in season.

If you suspect your doe to be in season, rubbing her back or flanks will often confirm this, as she will lift her rear end and flap her ears in response if she is in season.

If the doe is suspected to be in season she should be placed with the buck. If the buck is living with other bucks he should be removed and placed, with the doe, in a

When the doe is in season, she will be noticeably more active.

separate cage, as to introduce a doe to a cage of bucks can cause fighting between the bucks, and any, or all, of the bucks may mate with the doe.

The buck will sniff around the doe and, if she is in season, she will present herself to the buck by raising her rear, flapping her ears and allowing him to mate.

If the doe is not in season when placed with the buck, she will push him away when he tries to mate and may even squeal at him. The doe may be left with the buck, although he will try to mount her and she will reject his advances if she is not in season, but she should accept him within a few days when she does come

into season, and allow him to mate. Alternatively the doe and buck can be separated, returned to their usual cages and placed together on another evening when the doe is suspected to be in season.

THE MATING

The female will stand still, allowing mating to take place and the buck will mount and dismount several times. Inexperienced bucks may take a little while to start mating, or may attempt to mate from all angles, but generally they will understand what is required after a time! A buck is able to get the doe pregnant within a very short space of time and if mating continues for five to ten minutes there is a good chance that the mating has been successful. Inexperienced or young bucks may not get the doe pregnant first time and if no pregnancy results it may be necessary to do a repeat mating.

Once mating has taken place the buck and doe can be returned to their normal cages. If the buck used for mating lives with another buck or a group of bucks, they may sniff around the returning buck when he is placed in the cage. There may be some small

The buck should be returned to his cage after mating.

squabbles as the returned buck will have the doe's scent on him, but they should settle back happily together after a short time. If a buck has been removed for a long period of time (i.e. weeks) for mating, from the cage which he shared with another buck or group of bucks, it may not always be possible to return him to those cagemates. Therefore, the buck should only be removed for a short time if the intention is to return him to his original cagemates after mating.

If the doe was previously living with other does, she can also be returned to her cagemates after mating. The other does may follow her around the cage and sniff her, and there may be some slight squabbling as they re-assert their hierarchy of dominance, but peace and harmony will soon follow.

SIGNS OF PREGNANCY
A pregnant doe will often not come into season after a successful mating and this is one indication that a doe is pregnant. The doe may become less friendly towards you, preferring to spend time in her cage, and her nipples may become more prominent when she is pregnant.

THE PREGNANT RAT
At around 14-16 days after mating the rat may begin to appear pregnant, becoming swollen around the belly. Some does may not appear to be pregnant until much later. The pregnant doe

should be fed plenty of food, and a few treats such as carrot, bread soaked in milk, oat/bran mash, baby food or scrambled egg. Treats high in protein and fat and a few extra sunflower seeds will all help the doe through her pregnancy; vitamin drops in the water will also be beneficial at this time.

If a pregnant doe is dropped or squeezed, this can result in injury to the unborn babies or to the doe herself and, therefore, careful handling is required. It is usually wise to keep handling to a minimum once pregnancy has started to show. Removing the wheel during the latter part of pregnancy and while the mother is nursing will avoid excessive exercise and ensure that the doe does not neglect the litter.

PREPARING FOR THE BIRTH

You will need to consider the caging in which the doe is to give birth. Standard wire-barred cages are not ideal for a doe to give birth in as she may accidentally kick the babies through the bars of the cage and, as the babies grow older and start to explore, they can often squeeze between the bars and escape. An aquarium, or other solid-sided cage, is usually the best type of cage for birthing, as it is draught-proof, and helps to provide warmth for the mother and babies and does not allow the babies to be pushed out of the cage or enable them to escape when they are older.

If the doe shares a cage with other does this should not cause a problem, as the other does in the cage will often help the mother in caring for the litter, ensuring that the babies are kept warm when she is away from the nest. If several does have a litter at around the same time they may share the upbringing of all the babies in the cage between them. They will often place the babies from all the litters in one nest and take turns in nursing the babies or, if they keep their litters separate, they may take turns nursing their own and each other's litters. Often, if a doe is unable to nurse a litter, for example due to illness or death, another doe with a litter of similar age may nurse both litters and this has helped to ensure the survival of the rat in the wild. However, if you need to be certain which babies belong to which does, the pregnant does can be removed to separate cages. Introducing the does back into the main group, once the babies are weaned, may involve some initial squabbling as they re-establish dominance, but the group will usually settle again after a short while.

The gestation period for the rat is 21-23 days, and so counting this number of days from the mating will give the expected date of the arrival of the litter. Two days before this expected delivery date the cage should be cleaned, or the doe moved to a suitable birthing cage, and plenty of material should be provided with which the doe can build a nest in which to give birth. The doe should then be left quietly to prepare herself for the birth and be given plenty of food.

THE BIRTH

The doe will give birth to individual babies (known as kittens) at short intervals and may move around the cage while giving birth, leaving babies stranded in various corners of the cage. This is usually nothing to worry about as she will collect the babies together and take them to the nest once birthing is complete. There is likely to be some blood on the nesting material and this is quite normal and no cause for alarm. The babies are born without fur, are blind and deaf and weigh approximately five to six grams. As previously mentioned, the average litter size is eight but a doe can have up to 22 babies. However, although the doe only has 12 nipples, this does not present any problems with raising a larger litter.

Does usually come into season soon after giving birth and, if the buck has been left with the doe, he may mate again with the doe shortly after the birth. This does not give the doe adequate time between births to regain condition

The doe will give birth at short, regular intervals.

and can result in poorly-conditioned babies. It can also have a detrimental effect on the doe – it may affect her health and weight – so the buck must be removed before the doe gives birth.

INSPECTING THE LITTER

You should resist the temptation to inspect the litter, however curious you are. The mother should be disturbed as little as possible, particularly during the first week. She should be fed plenty of food, along with some bread soaked in milk, oat/bran mash, baby food, a few extra sunflower seeds and some healthy tidbits. The babies are likely to be covered by the nesting material and so you may not be able to see them, but do not be tempted to disturb the nest to have a look, as this is likely to upset the mother. The doe will be preoccupied in caring for her litter and may be a little aggressive towards you, so handling should be kept to a minimum during this time.

CARING FOR THE LITTER

The babies should not be touched or the nest disturbed for two weeks. If you touch the babies before this time you may upset the

mother by changing the scent of the babies. If it is necessary to pick up a baby, say, for example, if one has been left out of the nest for some time and the mother has not recovered it, or the baby has somehow been pushed outside the cage, this is best done by scooping the baby up with a spoon that has been wiped in some wood shavings from the cage. If the babies are to be dark-coloured

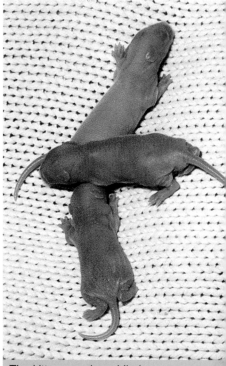

The kittens are born blind, deaf, and without fur.

rats, the skin will pigment at around three to six days and hair will begin to grow shortly afterwards.

The babies will start to run around the cage at around 10 to 14 days and the mother will usually retrieve them and take them back to the nest. The mother will pick the runaway babies up in her mouth, often by the scruff of the neck, but sometimes it may be by a leg or whatever she can get hold of to take them back to the nest. This is often met by vocal objections from the babies but does not usually result in injury. At this time the mother may endlessly be collecting runaway babies, returning one to the nest only to find another baby has decided to explore its surroundings. It is no easy task bringing up a large litter! The babies will have started to eat solid food and a shallow dish of bread soaked in milk, scrambled or boiled egg, oat/bran mash or baby food will easily be eaten by the growing youngsters.

By the time the babies are 14-16 days old, their eyes will have opened and the mother will have become more settled. This is the ideal time to start handling the young rats and the best way is simply to place your hand in the

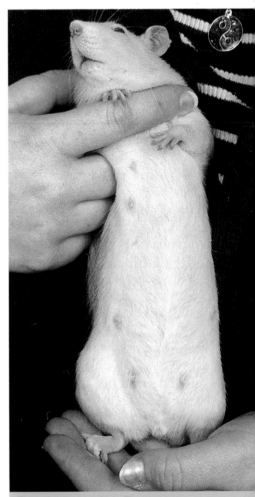

The nursing mother: The average size of litter is eight, but larger numbers are not unusual.

cage and allow them to sniff and climb over your hand. You can then progress to holding the baby rats for a short amount of time each day.

WEANING

At three to four weeks of age the babies are fully weaned and can be removed from the mother and placed into a cage of their own. It is a good idea to remove the babies into two cages at this time – one for bucks and one for does to avoid breeding of brothers and sisters at such an early age. Again, care should be taken over the choice of cage as the babies may squeeze though the bars of a typical rat cage. Aquariums are ideal for baby rats, being draught and escape-proof, and providing more warmth than a standard cage. If cage space is limited, the young does can be kept with the mother and the young bucks moved to a separate cage.

The babies should continue to be fed an abundance of rat mix or pellets, together with continued feeding of bread soaked in milk, oat/bran mash, baby food and tidbits such as carrots or scrambled or boiled egg. Do not feed too much green food, however, as this could cause diarrhoea at this stressful time; a little now and again is sufficient. Once the young rats have settled away from the mother, handling of the youngsters can be increased in order for the rats to become more confident about human contact. Avoid sudden movements as these will startle the young rats. Young rats, being very inquisitive, usually accept being handled quite readily and, if it is done gently, do not often nip.

The young rats will start to lose

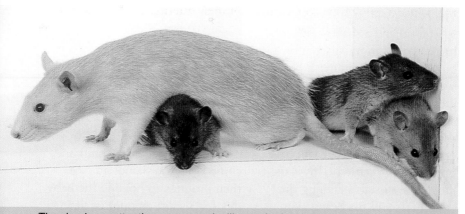

The doe is an attentive parent and will care for her kittens until they are weaned.

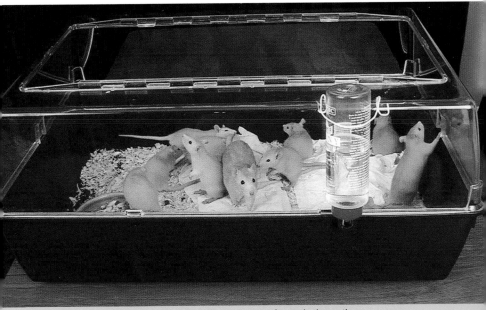

At four weeks, the kittens can be housed away from their mother.

their baby coat and grow their adult coat, which is a little harsher and may be slightly different in colour. At five to six weeks of age the baby rats should be confident, should happily accept being handled and be mature enough to go to new homes. They should not be given new homes before this time as they need the continuity of care, and the contact of their littermates, to avoid stress and to develop their confidence.

6 *Showing Rats*

The best way to start showing rats is to join a Rat, Rodent or Pet Club. Your library, your local pet store, or friends who already have rats may be able to help you find a club. Of course some clubs now have pages or sites on the Internet and it is possible to search the worldwide web for a list of rat clubs. Even if it is not your intention to enter into the world of showing rats, Rat, Rodent and Pet Clubs usually issue members with regular newsletters or journals and provide rat owners

It is a good idea to start showing in the pet classes. This doe is mis-marked, but would not be penalised in a pet class where the exhibits are judged on condition and tameness.

with the opportunity to contact other owners or breeders for advice. They are a good way of learning more about rats, gaining expert advice on their care and keeping up to date with the colours available.

Most clubs hold regular shows and these will consist of main classes for the more experienced exhibitors. The main classes usually encompass different classes for different colours and coat types; for example, there may be a class for Siamese Rats, Rex Rats, Variegated Rats, etc. Shows usually also have classes for Junior and Novice exhibitors. Most shows will also have a Pets Class, which is ideal for the first-time exhibitor.

In the main classes the rats are judged against written Standards, which set out what the ideal rat of a particular colour or type should look like, and it is against these Standards that rats in the main classes are assessed. There are written Standards for most of the colours, patterns and coat types available. The Standards also, normally, include guidance on the shape and build of the rat (often referred to as 'type'), as well as size, condition, fur and eyes and ears.

In the pets class the rats are judged solely on overall tameness and condition and need not be of a particular colour or variety, or fit exactly to the written Standards that apply to the main classes. You will often be able to speak to the judge afterwards and find out whether they think your rat is of a good enough quality to enter the main classes and be judged against the written Standards.

Clubs normally notify their members about shows, and give details of how to enter their rats and the show rules that apply in advance. They may also advertise locally in pet stores, or local papers, or on the Internet, with details of forthcoming shows and of how to enter your rat.

PREPARING FOR THE SHOW

Most clubs require you to enter your rat in advance rather than on the day of the show so, if you see a rat show advertised, you should contact the organisers and enter your rat beforehand. Clubs usually issue members with a show schedule (setting out the venue, time, classes and entry details) in advance. You should ensure that your rat is in good condition and free from any illness or infection prior to entering it into any show.

In the main classes, rats are judged against a written Standard, and exhibits must conform as closely as possible to the 'ideal' specimen described.

Any rats that are ill are liable for disqualification, and taking a rat that is out of condition to a show could cause it to become ill, or it could spread disease or illness among rats belonging to other exhibitors.

Many clubs require rats to be shown in special show tanks (plastic tanks with a sliding wire lid), particularly when entering your rat in the main classes. If you do not have one, you may be able to hire a show tank for the day from the club. Show tanks are used because they ensure that the owner of each rat remains anonymous to the judge, they provide an easy-to-open container which helps the judge in the task of assessing the rat, and they limit the space needed for the rats to be displayed on the judging tables.

If you are entering your rat in the pets class you may be able to show it in its own cage, or in a travelling container if the cage is too large to take to the show.

You will need to check beforehand, when you enter your rat into the show, whether you are required to show your rat in a show tank or are allowed to show it in its own cage. If a show tank is required, you can book this when entering your rat. These details are normally given on the show schedule.

You should also check whether any items are required, or are not allowed, in the show tank or cage. Some clubs require a piece of 'green food' to be placed in the show tank if the rat does not have access to water during the day, while other clubs may allow water bottles to be fixed to the show tanks. Rats entered in their own cage in the pets class are normally allowed all their usual accessories – bedding, food and water bottle may remain in the cage. Different clubs may have different rules.

THE DAY OF THE SHOW

On the day of the show, check your rat over and make sure that it appears well and clean. As mentioned previously, if your rat appears unhappy or unwell it should not be taken to the show – it could worsen your rat's

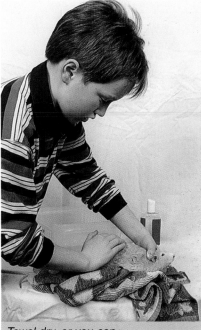

Towel dry, or you can use a hair-dryer.

Baby shampoo should be used when bathing your rat before a show.

condition, spread illness at the show to rats belonging to other exhibitors and could be disqualified by the judge.

Many exhibitors bath their rats on the morning of a show to ensure that the coats are clean and the rat is looking its best. This is best done by placing the rat in a shallow bowl of lukewarm water, or in a very shallow bath and gently soaking the rat. The coat can then be washed, using mild baby shampoo, before being rinsed thoroughly with clean,

The tail can be cleaned using a toothbrush.

put in the rat. If you are entering your rat in the pets class, you will need to prepare the cage by cleaning it and placing clean wood shavings and bedding inside, replenishing food, etc. When travelling to the show it is a good idea to remove the water bottle from your rat's cage, as the motion of moving the cage, whether you are walking, or going by train or car, will cause the bottle to drip and the cage floor to become wet – but remember to take it with you to the show, as you will want to fix it to the cage when you get there. If you have a long journey to the show, place some cucumber or carrot in the

lukewarm water. It is important that the rat is dried immediately to avoid it catching a chill. This can either be done using a towel, or by using a hairdryer set on a cool setting and held a good distance from the rat to avoid overheating. Make sure that the rat is kept warm once it has been dried.

If you are entering your rat into one of the main classes, prepare the show tank by placing a layer of wood shavings on its floor, place a piece of vegetable in the tank (if this is allowed), and finally

Make sure you have everything ready for the show.

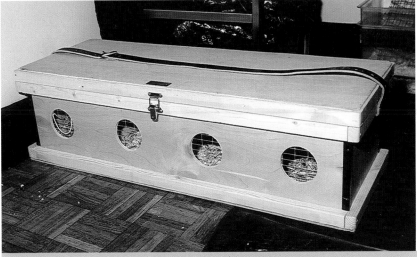

A travelling box designed for transporting show rats.

cage to compensate for the rat not having access to water during travelling.

Each rat will require a pen label – this is a label with an identification number to stick onto your cage or show tank which indicates the classes in which the rat is to be entered. If you have received these in the post beforehand you should stick them to the show tank or cage. If you are showing your rat in its cage, the pen label should be stuck to the side of the cage. If showing in a show tank, the label is normally stuck on the top of one of the narrow sides of the tank. You should make a note of the identification number on the label

so that you can easily find your rat at the end of a show. It is amazing how much alike several rats of the same colour can look when they are all placed in show tanks, and finding your own beloved pet among them at a large show may not be as easy as it sounds!

Ensure that you have everything you need for the show – a copy of the show schedule, a pen, some spare pieces of vegetables and, of course, your rat, and set off, allowing plenty of time to arrive before judging is due to start.

On arrival at the show, if you have not already received your pen labels, or paid for your entries, or if you have hired a show tank, you will need to go to the show

The show tank is clearly marked with your entry number.

secretary, who will deal with all of this. If, for some reason, you have not brought a rat that has been entered into the show, or you wish to change the classes your rat is entered into, you should notify the show secretary so that the paperwork for the judge can be amended before the show starts. The show secretary will also tell you where to place your cage or show tank to await judging.

THE JUDGING PROCEDURE
The judge is usually helped by stewards. These are volunteers who will place the tanks of rats for each class on the judging table, place them in order of marks once judged and then place them back on the main tables once judging of the class has finished. As each class is judged, the stewards will collect the rats for the next class and place them on the judging table.

In the main classes the judge will be looking for a rat that is a good example of the colour, of good build, size and condition, with good fur, and will judge the rat according to Standards written for the variety, or colour, and award marks. The rats for each class will be placed on the judging table and the judge will remove each rat from its show tank or cage in order to assess it and mark it against the written Standards. As the judge considers the rat, he or she will allocate marks and

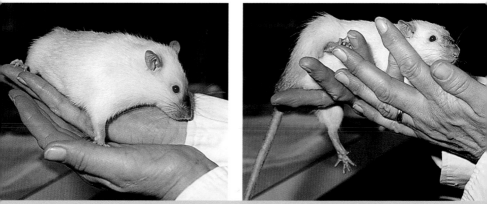

The judge will remove each rat from its show tank in order to judge it.

make comments about the rat and a steward will fill in a judging form with the marks and comments given by the judge. The marks for each category under which the rat is judged are then added together to give a total overall mark for the rat.

As each rat is judged and awarded marks they will be lined up on the judge's table in order, according to the total points awarded to each rat, and at the end of each class the rats with the highest points will be awarded places. Clubs vary as to the number of places they award. The judge may use coloured stickers to indicate the rats that have been placed in each class, which are stuck on the show tanks once judging of the class is complete.

At the end of the show the

The judge will give each rat a detailed examination in order to assess coat, colour, conformation and overall condition.

judge will normally award a Best In Show – this is the rat that has the highest number of points awarded across all of the main classes. There may also be other overall awards, such as Best Adult, Best Kitten, etc.

In the pets class the judge will be looking for an animal in good condition with a nice temperament. The judge will remove each rat from its cage in turn in order to assess it and will award marks accordingly, before deciding a winner.

During judging, exhibitors should not do anything that could indicate to the judge that they own a particular rat – this could result in the rat being disqualified.

Once judging has been completed most judges will be happy to discuss any questions you may have about your rat. If you wish to breed better rats this is a good opportunity to find out what you should be aiming for in your breeding. However, the judge should not be disturbed while judging is taking place and so, if you do have any questions, you should wait until all the competition has been completed.

Often clubs will welcome volunteers to act as stewards and so, if you wish to learn more about judging and see how it is carried out, you should ask the show secretary if you could help with stewarding. There will usually be an experienced steward who will teach you and help you if it is your first time.

7 Health Care

Rats are quite hardy pets but can be prone to respiratory problems. If a rat does become ill, it can deteriorate quickly and so, if the condition of your rat does not improve within a couple of days, or it deteriorates, veterinary treatment should be sought as soon as possible. The most common sign that a rat is sick is a red or black discharge around the eyes and nose, due to a red pigment in the rat's mucous membranes.

ABSCESSES
Abscesses usually occur when a bite or cut becomes infected and pus builds up under the skin. Often the bite or cut may have healed by the time the swelling is noticed. A vet will be able to drain the abscess and apply medication, or administer antibiotics, to prevent the cut becoming re-infected and to help healing.

ALLERGY
If the rat has started sneezing and this is accompanied by excessive scratching or skin soreness and there are no sign of mites, it may be that your rat is allergic to something in its environment. Consider whether anything has been changed such as wood shavings, bedding material, etc. which could have caused an allergic reaction in your rat. Cedar shavings can cause allergic reactions in rats so should be avoided. Shavings from hardwood, or paper-based shavings are preferable. If an allergic reaction is suspected, the source will need to be identified and removed. If the symptoms are extreme, veterinary treatment may be needed.

BLOOD IN URINE
Blood in the urine can be caused by bladder infections or kidney problems and veterinary advice should be sought immediately, as

A healthy rat is alert and inquisitive.

antibiotic treatment may be needed.

BRAIN TUMOURS (WALTZING)
Sometimes (rarely) rats may develop a brain disorder that causes the rat to continually run in small circles. The symptoms usually occur at a young age and the rat is unable to run straight. These rats are sometimes referred to as 'Waltzing Rats' and, unfortunately, the disorder is untreatable, so any rat suffering a brain disorder should be humanely destroyed by a vet.

BROKEN LIMBS
Rarely, a rat may fall and break a limb, or break its tail in an accident. Unfortunately, because of their relatively small size, and the fact that a rat would chew any cast put on the leg, there is nothing that can be done – it is not possible to put a plaster cast on a rat's leg! The limb or tail will, however, heal itself given time, although it may not heal straight, but this does not normally inconvenience the rat. If a broken limb is suspected, remove the wheel from the cage and, if possible, place the rat in an aquarium so that exercise is kept to a minimum, feed a diet high in calcium and let the limb heal naturally.

CANCERS/TUMOURS
Rats can suffer from cancers and tumours but these are often treatable. The rat develops a hard lump, which will continue to increase in size. External tumours can often be successfully surgically removed. Internal tumours may not be treatable. Early referral to a vet is vital to increase the chance of successful treatment.

COLDS/SNEEZING

Not all sneezing is indicative of a cold. An allergy to wood shavings or dust, or sudden changes in temperature, can all cause sneezing. The occasional sneeze is usually nothing to worry about but continued sneezing, or sneezing with other symptoms, such as runny eyes, breathing difficulties or general poor appearance, is usually a sign that something is wrong.

Rats can catch colds from humans and so, if you have a cold or flu, you should keep the handling of your rat to a minimum until you are recovered. If your rat does have a cold the symptoms are a runny nose, runny eyes and sneezing and the rat may wheeze and/or have difficulty breathing. The rat should be kept in a warm room of constant temperature and, if not recovered in a day or two or if its condition worsens, should be taken to a vet who may administer antibiotic treatment.

CONSTIPATION

Rats can suffer from constipation; the rat may walk 'hunched up' as if in pain and there will be a lack of droppings in the cage. The rat may also have problems passing droppings and may seem uncomfortable. If constipation is suspected, feed some green food and, if there is no improvement within a day, take the rat to a vet for treatment.

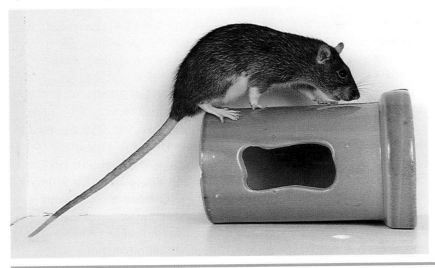

CUTS AND WOUNDS

Most cuts and wounds will heal by themselves but serious wounds should be monitored and the rat taken to a vet if any sign of infection occurs. Sometimes wounds can become infected, resulting in an abscess.

DIARRHOEA

The symptoms of diarrhoea are light-coloured, soft droppings which can be accompanied by wetness or dirtiness around the anus. The most common cause of diarrhoea is the overfeeding of green or soft food, or a sudden change in diet. In the event of diarrhoea you should cease feeding green food immediately, giving only the basic rat mix or pellets, and, if the rat is not recovered in a day or two, it should be taken to a vet, as antibiotic treatment and anti-diarrhoea treatment may be needed. Green food can be re-introduced to the diet gradually once the rat has recovered and gained any weight that was lost due to the diarrhoea.

FUR LOSS

Fur loss can occur in youngsters where both parents are Rex rats. The fur often regrows within a few weeks but may be sparse; the breeding of Rex to Rex is therefore not advised. A rat's fur may become thinner during periods of moult or as the rat becomes older. However, any excessive fur loss, or fur loss accompanied by irritation, scratching, soreness, scabs or flakiness of skin should be checked out by a vet as it may be an indication of mites, an allergy or a skin infection.

LONG NAILS

Occasionally rats may develop long toenails, which can often result in scratches as the rat washes itself. This can be helped by letting the rat run on sandpaper for short periods, or by filing the nails. The nails may require clipping and this is best done by a vet or experienced rat owner to avoid cutting the nails too short and injuring the rat.

LOSS OF LIMB/TAIL

Sometimes a rat may have a limb or its tail missing. This can be due to accident or to genetic deformity. If the limb or tail is missing due to an accident the rat should be taken to a vet, who may prescribe antibiotics to ensure that no infection occurs. Any rat with a limb or tail missing due to genetic

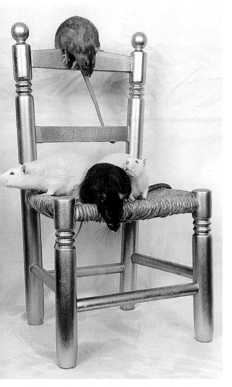

cases the rat may also have a nasal discharge. The rat should be taken to a vet who will usually be able to administer antibiotics to clear up the infection.

MITES
Occasionally rats may catch mites, most often from hay infected with mites – these may be seen moving on the coat of the rat and the rat may scratch more than usual and have bald spots. Mites can be transferred from one rat to another and so any rat suspected of having mites should be isolated. Minor cases of mites can be treated with an anti-mite spray, intended for birds or small animals and sold in pet stores, but care should be taken not to spray into the rat's eyes. In severe or prolonged cases of mites, veterinary advice should be sought .

deformity should not be bred from, as the genetic deformity could be passed on to any babies. Most rats will manage perfectly adequately with one limb missing, or their tail missing, and will still lead an active life.

MIDDLE EAR INFECTION
An infection of the middle ear causes the rat to hold its head to one side and walk in circles (similar to the symptoms of a stroke or 'Waltzing'). In extreme

RESPIRATORY PROBLEMS / LUNG INFECTIONS
It should be remembered that domestic rats are not as resistant to damp and cold as the wild variety, and this can lead to respiratory problems. This type of problem is quite common in domestic rats and the symptoms are often sneezing accompanied by

Check your rat each week for signs of illness.

RINGTAIL

Ringtail is caused when the atmosphere is too dry i.e. less than 50 per cent humidity. The tail becomes narrowed and then swells around the base. The humidity should be increased or the tail may be lost.

SHOCK

Sometimes a rat may injure itself and become shocked – the rat may shiver or lie still, breathing heavily. Keep the rat quiet and dark, cover the cage with a towel or cup the rat in your hands, shielding out light. If the rat is not recovered in a few minutes or its condition worsens, it may be necessary to take it to the vet.

STROKES

Rats can suffer from strokes and, although they usually occur in older rats, they do sometimes affect younger rats. These happen most often at night and so the first sign is when, the following morning, the rat is unbalanced and, typically, the head tilts to one side. The symptoms are similar to those of Middle Ear Infection (see above) and so veterinary advice should be sought to confirm. A rat which has suffered a stroke

wheezing and a red discharge from the nose. Any rat showing these signs of illness should be taken to a vet immediately for antibiotic treatment.

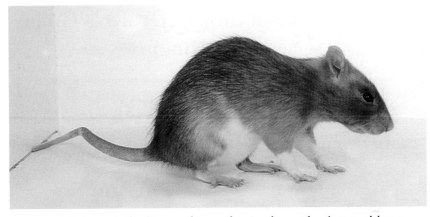

may need help with feeding and drinking due to the loss of co-ordination but should recover sufficiently after a week or two to feed itself. Rats who have suffered strokes usually improve over time and may live quite a while longer and lead fairly normal lives, although some head tilt may remain.

TOOTH PROBLEMS

As a rat's teeth are continually growing, there may, occasionally, be problems with the teeth overgrowing, or a chipped or broken tooth may result in the opposite tooth overgrowing. Teeth problems can result in weight loss due to the rat having problems eating. Overgrown teeth should be treated and a vet will be able to clip the teeth down to the correct length. Feeding dog biscuits, or providing the rat with something to gnaw, will help to prevent teeth from overgrowing. Sometimes older rats may have a tooth that grows crooked and this may result in the teeth overgrowing and may need regular clipping.

VAGINAL BLEEDING (DOES)

Vaginal bleeding (other than the beginning of labour) can indicate uterine problems and early veterinary treatment should be sought.

OTHER TITLES IN THE SERIES

Also available in the Pet Owner's Guide series from Ringpress

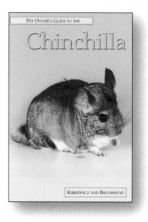

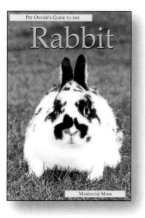

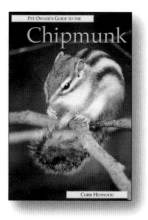

For a complete list of Britain's best pet books, write to:
**Ringpress Books, P.O. Box 8, Lydney, Gloucestershire, GL15 4YN.
Tel 01594 845577   Fax 01594 845599**